Hand Evaluation: Points, Schmoints!

Guaranteed to make
YOU
a Better Bidder

By Marty Bergen

Marty Bergen

Bergen Books

Thanks To:

Layout, cover design, and editing by
Hammond Graphics.

My very special thanks to: Cheryl Angel,
Cheryl Bergen, Gary Blaiss, Caitlin, Larry Cohen,
Nancy Deal, Ned Downey, Pete Filandro, Jim Garnher,
Lynn and Steve Gerhard, Pat Harrington, Steve Jones,
Doris Katz, Al Kimel, Alex Martelli,
Harriet and David Morris, Phyllis Nicholson,
David Pollard, Mark Raphaelson, Jesse Reisman,
Jeff Rubens, Bill Sachen, Maggie Sparrow,
Tom Spector, Merle Stetser, and Bobby Stinebaugh.

The Secrets of Winning Bridge by Jeff Rubens

Bergen Books
9 River Chase Terrace
Palm Beach Gardens, FL 33418-6817

First Printing: November, 2002

Library of Congress Control Number: 2002095649

ISBN 0-9716636-5-3

Bridge Books by Marty Bergen

Understanding 1NT Forcing

Marty Sez

Marty Sez...Volume 2

POINTS SCHMOINTS!

More POINTS SCHMOINTS!

Introduction to Negative Doubles

Negative Doubles

Better Bidding with Bergen, Volume I

Better Bidding with Bergen, Volume II

Everyone's Guide to the New Convention Card

**For information on ordering books
and CDs from Marty,
please refer to pages 63-64.
GREAT DISCOUNTS!**

**To order, call
1-800-386-7432**
or email: mbergen@mindspring.com

Contents

FYI 6

Hand Evaluation Glossary 7

Honor Cards

The True Value of Honor Cards 8

Quick Tricks 9

Honors in Your Long Suit(s) 10

Honors in Your Short Suit(s) 11

Honors in Partner's Long Suit 12

Proven and Unproven Honors 13

Honors in Partner's Short Suit 14

Honors in the Opponent's Suit(s) 15

The Very Useful Fourth Card 16

Overcoming the Block 17

Distribution

8 Trumps vs. 9 18

Your Distribution in the Side Suits 19

After Opener Raises Your Suit 20-21

Length in the Opponent's Suit 22

Shortness in the Opponent's Suit 23

The Wonders of Voids 24

After Partner's Limit Raise 25

Splinter Bids 26-29

4-3-3-3 is a Terrible Distribution 30-31

5-4-3-1 is Underrated 32

Length After Partner's 1NT 33

Suit Quality

Counting Playing Tricks 34-35

100 honors 36

Appreciating Intermediates 37-39

A Helpful Review

A Penny for My Thoughts 40
Pluses and Minuses 41
Your Turn to Shine 42-43

Opener in Action

The Rule of 20 – with Adjustments 44
Dear Marty 45
Opener Has 4 Diamonds and 5 Clubs 46
Strong Enough to Open 2♣? 47
Opener Raises Responder's Major 48
Fits and Misfits 49
Should You Open 1NT? 50
After 1NT - 2NT 51
After Partner Transfers 52

Responder in Action

After Partner Opens 1NT 53
After Opener Rebids His Suit 54
I Changed My Mind 55
Raising Opener's Major 56
After Opener Raises Your Major 57
She Who Knows, Goes 58

A Few Last Evaluations

Responding to Partner's Double 59
Bigger May Not Be Better 60
Smaller May Be Better 61

Better Bridge with Marty

A Cruise with a Bonus 62
Recommended Books and CDs 63-64

FYI

1. The player with the bidding decision is indicated by three question marks: ??? For consistency, South is always that player, and his hand is the one displayed.

2. Every bidding diagram begins with West.

West	North	East	South
—	Pass	1♡	???

The dash is only a place holder. In this example, North is the dealer. The "—" does not indicate a "Pass."

3. RHO = right-hand opponent; LHO = left-hand opponent

Bidding Style Used in This Book

Opening Bid Style:
Five-card majors in 1st and 2nd seat.
Light opening bids, based on the Rule of 20.
Opening 1NT = 15-17 HCP. Opening 2NT = 20-21 HCP.
2♣ opening — strong, artificial and forcing.
Weak two-bids in diamonds, hearts, and spades.
Preempts may be light.

Responding:
Limit raises — all suits.
Jacoby Transfers and Stayman after notrump.

Slam Bidding:
Blackwood — traditional, not Roman Key Card.

Competitive:
Michaels Cue-Bid, Unusual Notrump.

Worth Knowing

Hand Evaluation – Judging the strengths and weaknesses of your hand to determine its trick-taking capability.

Hand Reevaluation – Revaluating your hand based on the bidding by any of the other three players.

Working Cards (Proven Values) – Honor cards which are "known" to be useful when evaluating your hand.

Prime Cards – Aces and kings.

Minor Honors (Soft Values) – Queens and jacks.

Quick Tricks – AK = 2, AQ = 1½, A = 1, KQ = 1, Kx = ½

Spot Cards – Any card from two through nine.

Intermediates – Tens and nines (and even eights).

Downgrading a Hand – When you determine that a hand is worth less than its point count would suggest.

Upgrading a Hand – When you determine that a hand is worth more than its point count would suggest.

Source of Tricks – A long or strong suit which is expected to produce several extra tricks.

Playing Tricks – The number of tricks you expect to win in your own hand. Only relevant if you have a long and strong suit, and you become declarer.

Playing Strength – A hand's trick-taking potential. Hands with good playing strength should be upgraded.

The True Value of Honor Cards

The 4-3-2-1 point count is not completely accurate. Aces are greatly underrated, while queens and jacks are definitely overrated.

Do not despair. No one is suggesting that you need to find another way to count your points. However, while 4-3-2-1 gets an A+ for easy-to-use, it rates only a B- for accuracy.

Can we do better? Bridge theorists, after years of study, have devised a new scale with the help of computers.

Honor	Traditional	Reality
Ace	4	4 $\frac{1}{2}$
King	3	3
Queen	2	1 $\frac{1}{2}$
Jack	1	$\frac{3}{4}$
Ten	0	$\frac{1}{4}$

Notice that the total for each suit is still 10.

Do I suggest that you memorize the numbers on the right, and begin using fractions? Of course not. We all got our fill of fractions in grade school. On the other hand, I don't think it would be unrealistic to use these (whole) numbers:

2 aces = 9 points   2 queens = 3 points   4 jacks = 3 points

Also note: 1 ace has the same value as 3 queens,
            or 1 queen and 1 king.

Good news: HCP will be counted in the traditional way in this book, but from time to time, I will refer back to what "The Computer Sez."

Quick Tricks

Counting quick tricks is essential for good hand evaluation.

For each suit:

AK = 2,   AQ = 1½,   A = 1,   KQ = 1,   Kx = ½

(Notice that jacks are never "quick.")

Counting quick tricks helps you appreciate the fact that **all honor cards have more potential when they are in combination with other honors.**

These hands have the identical distribution and 12 HCP.

♠ 6 3   ♡ K Q 4 2   ◇ A Q J 4   ♣ 7 5 2
♠ A J   ♡ K 6 4 2   ◇ Q 6 4 3   ♣ Q 5 2

With the first hand, open 1◇. You have 2½ quick tricks, with all five honors in your two longest suits. But don't open the second hand. You have only 1½ quick tricks, and the suits with isolated honors aren't worth much.

Always count your quick tricks. It helps you know if you have "good" points, or merely a handful of "schmoints."

Quick tricks are especially relevant when considering:

1. a penalty double. Avoid doubles based on "points."
2. A 2♣ opening on an unbalanced hand. You need at least as many quick tricks as losers.

By the way: Most hands that open one of a suit in first or second position have at least two quick tricks.

Upgrade These Honors

Honors in your long suit(s) are far more valuable than honors in shorter suits.

Hands with "strong" long suits are excellent.
Hands with "weak" long suits are often disappointing.

West	North	East	South
—	—	Pass	1♡
Pass	2♡	Pass	???

♠ 6 4　♡ A K 7 6 4　◇ 8　♣ A K 6 5 3
Bid 4♡. You need very little from partner, and you have enough playing strength to insist on game. Once partner promises heart support, you can expect to set up clubs and eventually win at least four club tricks.

♠ K 4　♡ A 7 6 4 2　◇ 8　♣ A K 6 5 3
Bid 3♣ to invite game. If responder has a minimum raise and bids 3♡, you will be content to play in a part-score.

♠ K 4　♡ A 7 6 4 2　◇ A　♣ K 7 6 5 3
Bid 3♣. This hand is weaker than the previous one, because your singleton ◇A will not develop anything. Even so, game is still possible.

♠ A K　♡ 7 6 4 3 2　◇ A　♣ K 7 6 5 3
Pass. This hand is clearly the weakest of the four. With only one honor in your two long suits, you don't have enough playing strength to make 4♡. **When in doubt, take a good look at the quality and quantity of your trumps.**

Downgrade These Honors

Honors in short suits (singleton or doubleton) should be devalued.

Sometimes, honors in your short suits are not very useful.
A doubleton AK won't build as many tricks as AKxxx,
or even AKxx or AKx, but you can be sure of winning both
honors. However, when you have a doubleton such as QJ,
no one is surprised if your honors turn out to be worthless.

Here are the least effective honors in short suits.
I strongly recommend subtracting one point for these:
Singleton: king, queen, or jack   **Doubleton:** QJ, Qx, Jx

The following holdings are not as bad, but they should
also be devalued. I don't *insist* that you subtract ½ point
(please Marty, no more fractions), but they're questionable.
Singleton: ace   **Doubleton:** AJ, KQ, KJ

By the way: If your partner *bids* your short suit containing
one or two honors, everything changes. And if he happens
to be both long and strong in your short suit, your
"liability" could turn into an asset.

Suppose you pick up a hand with ♡Jx. You subtract one
point, treating your ♡J as no better than a deuce, and await
developments. If partner's bidding promises four hearts,
you restore the ♡J to 1 HCP. And if partner opens 1♡,
promising five hearts (probably with some heart strength),
you can upgrade your jack to 2 HCP.

Help for Partner

Honors in partner's long suit(s) are worth their weight in gold.

Once partner has shown a five-card suit, you should add
a point for any honor (above the 10) in his suit.
The maximum addition per hand is two points.

Also worth knowing:

- No bonus for a singleton honor unless partner has
  shown at least a six-card suit.

- If partner has shown two long suits, you get
  bonus points for honors in each one.

- Opposite a six-card suit, the ace or king is
  invaluable. Take a second point for either one.

Partner opens 1♠. What is your hand worth now?

♠ J   ♡ A Q 7 2   ◇ Q 6 4 2   ♣ 10 6 4 3
9 points. Unless partner rebids spades, don't add a point
for the *singleton* ♠J.

♠ Q 8 6   ♡ 8 5   ◇ A 8 7 5   ♣ 9 6 5 2
8 points. In addition to 6 HCP and a doubleton,
you are entitled to add a point for the ♠Q.

♠ K 10 3   ♡ A 9 7 5 3   ◇ 8 6   ♣ A 5 2
13 points. 11 HCP plus one for the doubleton, and you can
add one for the ♠K. The ♠10 is nice to have, but don't
add a point for it.

Location, Location, Location

Honors in partner's suit(s) are working cards.
In all other suits, only aces are proven.
Side queens and jacks are especially dubious.

"Working" and "proven" describe honor cards that are
likely to be useful for partner. "Cover cards" is another
term that is sometimes used because they "cover" losers.

West	North	East	South
Pass	1♠	Pass	???

♠ 5 4 2 ♡ K J 5 3 ◇ Q J 4 2 ♣ Q J
Despite your 10 HCP, a raise to 2♠ is enough.
Your six honor cards are all unproven.

♠ K Q 2 ♡ 8 6 4 2 ◇ A 6 5 3 ♣ 4 2
Because all three honors are proven, you are too strong to
bid 2♠. Whether your system calls for a bid of 2◇, 3♠,
or 1NT Forcing, this hand is worth a 3-card limit raise.

West	North	East	South
Pass	1♠	Pass	1NT
Pass	2♡	Pass	???

♠ 6 2 ♡ 10 8 6 4 ◇ K 7 6 2 ♣ K J 3
Pass. Chances for game are slim and none. Your three
minor-suit honors are unproven.

♠ K 2 ♡ K J 10 8 ◇ 8 7 6 2 ♣ 7 5 3
Bid 3♡ like a shot. All of your honors are working.

Wasted Honors

Honors in partner's short suit(s) are usually not worth much.

Honor cards are virtually worthless when partner is void in that suit; even an ace becomes a questionable card. If partner has a singleton, your ace is not wasted, but it won't help you develop additional tricks. Honors in partner's long suits are working because they build tricks. Honors in partner's short suits might as well be on vacation.

How do you know when partner has a short suit?
He shows one when he:

- Doubles for takeout.
- Makes a splinter bid.
- Bids a suit after your Jacoby 2NT response.
- Bids the other three suits.
- Overcalls the Unusual Notrump or Michaels (showing **two** short suits).

West	North	East	South
—	—	—	Pass
1♡	Dbl	Pass	???

♠ K 7 6 5 2   ♡ K Q 4   ◇ 6 4 3   ♣ 7 2
Bid only 1♠. Since partner is short in hearts, your heart honors will not be worth much.

♠ K 7 6 5 2   ♡ 6 4 3   ◇ K Q 4   ♣ 7 2
Jump to 2♠. Partner's takeout double promises spades, diamonds, and clubs, so all your honors are working.

Honors in the Opponent's Suit(s)

Aside from the ace, upgrade honors in RHO's suit, but downgrade honors in LHO's suit.

Use the opponents' bidding to evaluate your hand. Your honor cards are more likely to win tricks when the opponents' strength is "in front of" you (on your right). On the other hand, if the opponents' strength is "behind" you (on your left), your honors may have very little trick-taking potential.

You are South, with this indifferent collection — 6 HCP and flat as a pancake.

♠ K 7 2   ♡ K 8 5   ◇ 8 6 4 3   ♣ 9 5 2

West	North	East	South
1♣	1♠	2♡	???

Bid 2♠. Your ♡K is looking good behind the heart bidder (East). With two proven honors, you are delighted to raise.

However, with the same hand after:

West	North	East	South
1♡	1♠	2♣	???

Pass. Now you're sitting in front of the heart bidder (West), so the ♡K is *very* questionable.

Bridge is Better When You Have a Fourth

With several honors in one suit, the difference between three and four cards is significant, even when the fourth card is a deuce.

It is easy to appreciate your small cards with a long, strong suit such as KQJ32. It is also easy to regret the lack of small cards when you have a doubleton such as KJ. However, not everyone realizes how much better it is to hold a suit such as AKQ2 compared to AKQ.

With AKQ2, you have prospects for a fourth trick, even if partner has three small cards. Opposite xxxx, you can expect to win a fourth trick. Obviously, if partner has J or Jx or Jxx, a fourth winner is guaranteed. When you hold only AKQ, even if partner has Jxxx or Jxxxx, you'll have to cope with a blocked suit.

What other suits with two or three honors have a great deal more potential when they contain a fourth card? EVERY SINGLE ONE OF THEM.

Whether your 4-card suit includes 3 big honors (AKQx) or 3 smaller honors (even the QJ10x), ya gotta love that fourth card.

Whether your 4-card suit includes 2 big honors (AKxx) or 2 smaller honors (even the J10xx), you love the fourth card.

Speaking of AKQ reminds me of one of my favorite lesson hands (see next page). Would you make 3NT?

Contract: 3NT
Lead: ♡Q

North
♠ Q 3 2
♡ K 5 3
♢ J 5 4 2
♣ K J 3

West
♠ A 7
♡ Q J 10 6
♢ 9 7 6 3
♣ A 7 5

East
♠ K 8 6 4
♡ 9 8 7 2
♢ 10 8
♣ 8 6 2

South
♠ J 10 9 5
♡ A 4
♢ A K Q
♣ Q 10 9 4

West	North	East	South
—	Pass	Pass	1NT
Pass	2NT	Pass	3NT
All Pass			

North correctly downgrades his flat, aceless 10-count and only raises to 2NT, but South loves his intermediate cards in the black suits and carries on to game.

South sees nine tricks: four diamonds, two hearts and three clubs. But the blocked diamond suit is a problem. Most declarers win the ♡A, saving the ♡K as the entry to the ♢J. But, when they unblock diamonds and play clubs, if West holds up his ♣A, South has no entry to his last club!

South should win the ♡K at trick one, unblock diamonds and play clubs. One of dummy's club honors must provide the necessary entry to the ♢J.

Eight "Never," Nine Ever

With weak trumps and only an 8-card fit, don't be pushy. But with a suitable hand and a *ninth* trump, you should push for a major-suit game.

We all learned that "eight is enough," and sometimes it is. However, on many distributional hands, eight trumps is not enough to allow declarer to do everything he needs to do.

West	North	East	South
—	—	—	1♠
Pass	2♠	Pass	???

♠ J 7 6 5 4   ♡ 5   ◇ A K 5 4   ♣ K Q J

Pass. If partner has exactly three trumps, he would need to have the perfect hand to make a game. **Marty Sez:** "He who seeks perfect dummy need only look in mirror."

♠ J 7 6 5 4 3   ♡ 5   ◇ A K 5   ♣ A 10 3

Bid 3♣. The extra trump makes all the difference in the world. Your second choice is 4♠, not pass.

West	North	East	South
—	—	—	1♠
Pass	1NT	Pass	2♡
Pass	3♡	Pass	???

♠ A K J 8 2   ♡ J 7 4 3   ◇ K J 7   ♣ 3

Pass. Weak trumps, not to mention too many jacks.

♠ A 8 6 5 4   ♡ J 7 4 3 2   ◇ A Q   ♣ 3

Bid 4♡. On *this* auction, opener should bid 4♡ whenever he has a fifth heart.

Got Anything Going on the Side?

In a suit contract, when you have a long suit, your distribution in the other suits is still very relevant. Balanced is boring.

Everyone loves to pick up a long suit, as well they should. Just don't forget to consider the rest of your distribution. **Hands with long suits are much more effective in a suit contract when accompanied by very short suit(s).**

Boring	Not Bad	Very Good	Awesome
5-3-3-2	5-4-2-2	5-4-3-1	5-4-4-0
6-3-2-2	6-3-3-1	6-4-2-1	6-4-3-0
7-2-2-2	7-3-2-1	7-4-1-1	7-4-2-0

Suppose you pick up a nice 6-card suit. Sounds good, but how are your other suits distributed? It *does* matter.

West	*North*	*East*	*South*
Pass	1NT	Pass	2♡*
Pass	2♠	Pass	???

*Jacoby Transfer

♠ K Q 7 5 4 2 ♡ 6 4 ◇ J 10 ♣ 6 5 3
Pass. Game is very unlikely.

♠ K Q 7 5 4 2 ♡ 6 ◇ J 10 9 ♣ 6 5 3
Raise to 3♠. Things are looking up.

♠ K Q 7 5 4 2 ♡ 6 ◇ J 10 9 8 ♣ 6 5
Jump to 4♠. Looking good! 6-4, bid more.

After Opener Raises Your Suit

Before the auction begins, some players count for length. Others add points for short suits. Regardless:

Once partner raises your suit, trump length AND short suits are both relevant. You should add points for each of these assets.

Obviously, this assumes that you intend to play with the agreed suit as trumps, rather than notrump.

Points for Trump Length

5-card suit	add 1 point
6-card suit	add 3 points
7-card suit	add 5 points

Note: After the 5th card, each trump is worth 2 points. Once partner raises your suit, the traditional method of adding 1 point for each card beyond four is not sufficient.

Points for Short Suits

void = 3,   singleton = 2,   doubleton = 1

Very important note: The Computer Sez: the player who expects to become declarer should not add any points for his first doubleton.

Bonus for 2-Suiters

With 10+ cards in your two longest suits, add 1 point. **Note:** 5-5, 6-4, 7-3, 6-5, etc., all apply.

After Opener Raises (continued)

West	North	East	South
—	1♣	Pass	1♠
Pass	2♠	Pass	???

♠ A K 8 4 3   ♡ 5 4   ◇ J 7 6 5   ♣ 6 4

    8 HCP
    +1 trump length (5-card trump suit)
    +1 doubleton (ignoring first doubleton)
    ——
    10

Opener probably has fewer than 16 distribution points, so your side has fewer than 26. You should pass.

West	North	East	South
—	1♣	Pass	1♡
Pass	2♡	Pass	???

♠ 7 4   ♡ A J 7 6 4   ◇ K Q 2   ♣ J 9 4
11 HCP +1 (trump length) = 12
Ignore your first doubleton, adding no points for your spade holding. You have enough for an invitational raise to 3♡, but that's all.

♠ A 10 6 3   ♡ 9 8 6 5 4 2   ◇ K 9   ♣ 5
7 HCP + 3 (length) + 2 (singleton) + 1 (2-suiter) = 13
That's all you need to jump to 4♡.

♠ 4   ♡ K J 7 5 2   ◇ A 9 8 2   ♣ Q 8 4
10 HCP + 1 (length) + 2 (singleton) = 13. Bid 4♡.

Misplaced Length

Length in the opponent's suit is a huge liability, even if you have a fit with partner. When that opponent is sitting behind you, it's even worse.

West	North	East	South
—	1♦	Pass	1♠
2♣	2♠	Pass	???

♠ Q 5 4 2   ♡ Q 4   ♦ A J   ♣ K 7 6 5 3

Pass. What are you going to do with all your clubs? If you try to ruff some of them, East will overruff.

West	North	East	South
1♦	Dbl	1♠	2♡
Pass	Pass	3♣	???

♠ 7 5   ♡ Q 8 7 4 3   ♦ A Q 8 6 5   ♣ 2

Pass. Once West opened 1♦, your diamonds lost all their luster.

West	North	East	South
—	—	—	1♠
Dbl	3♠	4♡	???

♠ A K Q J 6   ♡ K J 8 4   ♦ J 3   ♣ K 7

Double. Your hearts will be more useful on defense.

By the way: These hands were taken from actual play. Each famous expert (South) ignored his "liability" and bid. In every case, bidding was 100% wrong. If I hadn't always been South's partner, I might even have been amused!

Shorter is Better

The shorter you are in the opponent's suit, the harder you should try to take action.

If RHO opens (any level), and you have a borderline hand, let your holding in his suit be your guide.

- With a singleton or void, almost anything goes.
- With a doubleton, you can go either way.
  Make your decision based on the vulnerability.
- With three or more cards, be cautious.

West	North	East	South
—	—	1♠	???

♠ — ♡ 10 8 6 5 ◇ A Q 9 7 5 ♣ K 9 6 2
Double. No second choice. In fact, if East opens 2♠, and you are vulnerable, you should still double.

♠ A 3 ♡ J 6 4 2 ◇ K Q J ♣ Q 9 8 7
Double only if not vulnerable. Not enough prime cards.

♠ Q 7 2 ♡ Q 8 6 4 ◇ K J 3 ♣ A J 4
Pass, regardless of vulnerability. Avoid takeout doubles of a major with 4-3-3-3.

♠ 3 ♡ A 7 4 2 ◇ 4 3 ♣ A J 7 6 3 2
Overcall 2♣, regardless of vulnerability. A singleton spade, 6-4, and two aces. What are you waiting for?

♠ Q 7 6 3 ♡ Q 5 ◇ K 4 ♣ A J 7 6 3
Pass, regardless of vulnerability. Four cards in RHO's suit and an indifferent 5-card suit — no thanks.

The Wonder of Voids

A void in the opponent's suit can be magical. When you have a void (and a fit), you can often make game or slam without a lot of HCP.

I can't tell you how many times I have heard a player say after the hand was over: "Making six. Slam was cold, but with only --- HCP, there was no way to get there. My void sure came in handy, though." Too little, too late.

Here's a hand from a prestigious invitational tournament. Despite having only 7 HCP, would you appreciate the magic of your void?

♠ K 10 9 5   ♡ —   ◇ 10 9 8 4 3   ♣ K J 8 2

West	North	East	South
—	—	—	Pass
1♡	2♣	3♡	???

Eight experts were faced with this decision. Some players jumped to 5♣, which ended the auction. Others were interested in spades, and made a responsive (takeout) double. Because partner held four nice hearts, the double ended the auction when partner passed.

Only three Souths appreciated the potential of their void and cue-bid 4♡. Partner now drove to the ice-cold 6♣.

For those who like to know, partner held:
♠ A 2   ♡ Q 10 6 5   ◇ A   ♣ A 10 7 6 5 4

Appreciating Short Suits after a Limit Raise

After partner makes a limit raise in your major:
1. Don't pass with a singleton or void.
2. Even with a big hand, don't try for slam without a short suit.

West	North	East	South
—	—	—	1♡
Pass	3♡	Pass	???

♠ 7 ♡ K Q 9 7 5 ◇ A Q 10 5 ♣ 8 5 3
Bid 4♡. Whether you were confident or nervous about opening this nice Rule of 20 hand, you should be delighted to accept partner's invitation based on your singleton.

♠ Q 7 ♡ A K Q J 3 ◇ J 7 5 ♣ J 6 3
Pass. The ugly 5-3-3-2 distribution and too many minor honors overrule the 14 HCP and strong trumps. This hand has a lot more minuses than pluses.

♠ K 2 ♡ K Q 8 4 3 ◇ 6 5 ♣ A Q 9 4
Bid 4♡. No short suit, but this hand is clearly strong enough to accept partner's invitation.

♠ Q J ♡ K Q J 10 8 4 ◇ A Q ♣ K J 6
Bid 4♡. You have no singleton, so forget about slam.

♠ A 7 ♡ A Q 7 6 5 2 ◇ A K 9 8 ♣ 8
Cue-bid 3♠. Because of your 6-4 distribution and controls, this excellent hand has a lot more potential than the previous example.

Splinter Bids

When you have a fit, one of the best conventions for evaluating slam chances is the splinter bid.

Let the buyer beware: One player's idea of an artificial splinter bid may sound like a natural bid to his partner. It is essential that you and partner discuss this convention.

What must you know about splinter bids?

1. Splinter bids guarantee a fit and show a singleton or void in the suit named. These bids are forcing to game, and suggest the possibility of slam.

2. All splinter bids are jumps. The most obvious splinter bids are double jumps. However, when a nonjump bid in a suit would be forcing, experienced partnerships also define some unnecessary jump bids as splinters.

3. The strength needed to splinter can be obtained by subtracting the points partner has promised from 26. If you open 1♣ and partner shows 6+ points with a response of 1♠, you need 20 distributional points to splinter.

4. Voids are rare, so assume that partner's splinter bid is based on a singleton. Splintering with a singleton honor is imperfect, but it's okay to splinter if that's the only flaw.

5. Almost all splinter bids are raises of partner's suit with 4-card support.

Splinter Bids (continued)

Here are a few examples:

Bidding **Typical hand for splinter bid**
by our side

1♠ - 4◇   ♠ K 5 4 2   ♡ A 8 6 4   ◇ 5   ♣ A J 5 3

Responder's splinter raise of opener's major is the most likely splinter bid.

1♣ - 1♡   ♠ 2   ♡ A J 6 4   ◇ A 10 5   ♣ A K J 10 3
3♠

1♠ - 2♡   ♠ A Q 8 6 4   ♡ K 9 7 5   ◇ K 9 8 4   ♣ —
4♣

2♣ - 2◇   ♠ 9 8 6 4 3   ♡ A 8 6 4   ◇ 9 7 5   ♣ 7
2♡ - 4♣

After partner opens 2♣, you don't need much strength for a splinter bid.

1♣ - 1♡   ♠ K J 3   ♡ A J 10 7 5 3   ◇ 6   ♣ A 4 2
2♡ - 4◇

The 4◇ jump is referred to as a "self-splinter," because the player making the splinter bid initiated the trump suit (hearts), as opposed to raising the suit that partner bid first. This "raise yourself" type of splinter bid is the exception rather than the rule.

After Partner Splinters

The ideal holding in partner's short suit is length and weakness.

Why weakness?
You prefer to have your honor cards in partner's longer suits, where they will be more useful in building tricks.

Why length?
Once partner is void and can ruff, your small cards in the suit become winning tricks – and the more the merrier. In addition, having length in partner's short suit means that you'll be short in the other suits and can trump *his* losers.

Best holdings in the suit partner splinters into:
4 or 5 cards with very little (if any) strength.
3 small cards is also an excellent holding.

Worst holdings in the suit partner splinters into:
Strength and shortness. If you hold a KQ doubleton, five of your HCP are now worthless, as is the doubleton, because it is a duplication of values. Both players have assets they are valuing that will not translate into extra tricks. You need to uncover this problem during the auction. After viewing dummy, it's too late.

By the way: Although your holding in partner's short suit is very relevant, make sure to consider your entire hand.

By the way #2: If opener shows a short suit on a Jacoby 2NT auction, responder should evaluate his hand the same way as if opener had made a splinter bid.

A Splinter Bid Leads to Slam

Contract: 6♠
Lead: ♠3

North
♠ Q J 7 2
♡ K 10 6
◇ Q
♣ A J 7 5 3

West
♠ 4 3
♡ J 7 5 3
◇ A J 5
♣ K 10 8 4

East
♠ 8
♡ Q 9 4 2
◇ K 10 8 7 6
♣ Q 6 2

South
♠ A K 10 9 6 5
♡ A 8
◇ 9 4 3 2
♣ 9

West	North	East	South
—	—	Pass	1♠
Pass	4◇	Pass	4NT
Pass	5◇	Pass	6♠
All Pass			

North's 4◇ bid was music to South's ears. His diamonds were no longer a liability. With South's extra trump and controls in hearts and clubs, slam prospects were rosy.

West made the best lead of a trump. South won the ♠9, and led the ◇2. West grabbed his ◇A, and led a second trump. Fortunately, South appreciated dummy's 5-card club suit. Declarer won the ♠J, cashed the ♣A and ruffed a club. He led clubs each time that dummy obtained the lead, and eventually discarded his ◇9 on North's last club.

29

Flat as a Pancake

Whether declaring or defending, in notrump or suit play, 4-3-3-3 distribution is awful. Hands with this shape should always be downgraded.

When your side declares a suit contract
A 4-3-3-3 hand can't ruff anything or set up a long suit.

When your side defends a suit contract
You'll never get a ruff, and you will be forced to obediently follow suit "forever." Avoid aggressive penalty doubles; declarer is likely to enjoy the play when he discovers that suits are evenly divided. Even if you have four strong trumps, you are likely to be endplayed if declarer refrains from drawing trumps.

When your side declares a notrump contract
4-3-3-3 hands have very limited trick-taking potential. Once you take your obvious winners, what do you do for an encore?

When your side defends a notrump contract
Trying to defeat a notrump contract without a long suit is no easy task.

Is there anything positive about a 4-3-3-3 hand?
Not much. They *are* usually easy to bid. In addition, if partner has a distributional hand, you can't have a misfit.

By the way: It is also worth noting that 5-3-3-2 distribution is overrated in suit contracts. I refer to these hands as "the 4-3-3-3 of 5-card suits."

Flat as a Pancake (continued)

North knew his side had at least 33 HCP, and jumped to 6NT. Unfortunately, 12 tricks were impossible.

North

Contract: 6NT
Lead: ♡10

♠ K Q J
♡ A Q 6
♢ 7 6 5 3
♣ A Q 2

West
♠ 8 5
♡ 10 9 8 7 3
♢ J 9
♣ 7 5 4 3

East
♠ 10 9 4 3 2
♡ J
♢ K Q 8 2
♣ 10 9 8

South
♠ A 7 6
♡ K 5 4 2
♢ A 10 4
♣ K J 6

West	North	East	South
—	—	Pass	1NT
Pass	6NT	All Pass	

In fact, when neither red suit divided 3-3, declarer was unable to take more than 10 tricks.

North's hand was not worth 18 HCP. Not only was he 4-3-3-3, but his 4-card suit was awful. With the equivalent of a 3-3-3-3 hand, some discretion was in order. North should have downgraded his hand and invited slam by bidding 4NT. With a 15-count and 4-3-3-3, South would have passed.

A Very Underrated Distribution

5-4-3-1 is a very underrated distribution for suit contracts. Unless the hand is a misfit, bid aggressively when you have this shape.

What's so good about it?

- Your 5-card suit provides a source of tricks
- Your singleton is a great asset
- You have three suits that you're willing to play in

West	North	East	South
—	—	Pass	1◇
Pass	1♠	Pass	???

♠ K Q 10 8 ♡ 6 ◇ A K 9 8 4 ♣ 6 5 3
Bid 3♠. Make a mental note to thank partner for bidding spades. Every one of your honor cards is a proven value.

♠ A Q 6 ♡ A 10 7 5 ◇ A Q 9 5 3 ♣ 6
Bid 2♡. With three aces and no signs of a misfit, you should upgrade your hand and reverse, even though you have "only" 16 HCP.

♠ A 9 8 ♡ 4 ◇ A Q J 9 7 ♣ A K 10 3
Bid 3♣. It's okay to jump-shift with *these* 18 HCP.

♠ K 10 7 2 ♡ A 6 4 ◇ A K J 10 8 ♣ 3
Bid 4♣ if you're playing splinter bids, or 4♠ if you're not. Regardless of your system, you should upgrade this hand and insist on game.

Length After Partner Opens 1NT

When partner opens 1NT, your long suits are wonderful assets. Upgrade hands which contain a suit of at least five cards.

Quantity Suggestions:
5-card suit	add 1 point
6-card suit	add 2 points

Quality Suggestions:
With a very weak suit (0 honors), subtract 1 point.
With a very strong suit (3+ honors), add 1 point.

West	North	East	South
Pass	1NT	Pass	???

♠ 8 4 ♡ 7 6 2 ◇ A K 10 9 5 ♣ 10 5 3
Raise to 2NT. Once you add two points for the 5-card suit headed by three honors, your nine points justify a raise.

♠ Q 4 ♡ A 7 2 ◇ 8 7 5 4 3 ♣ Q J 5
Bid only 2NT. All you have is 9 HCP, because your 5-card suit has no honors.

♠ 7 4 ♡ Q 6 2 ◇ K 8 5 4 3 ♣ A 5 2
Bid 3NT. After partner opens 1NT, hands with 9 HCP and a decent 5-card suit should insist on game.

♠ 8 6 4 ♡ K 6 ◇ 7 2 ♣ A J 10 7 6 5
Bid 3NT. 8 HCP + 2 (6-card suit) + 1 (3 honors) = 11.

♠ Q J 4 ♡ A 6 ◇ A J 6 ♣ K 10 9 7 5
Invite slam with 4NT. 15 HCP + 1(5-card suit) = 16.

Counting Playing Tricks

On most hands, you count your points, evaluate your hand, bid accordingly, and hope for the best. For example, you open 1NT, and partner invites game by raising to 2NT. You hold:

♠ A Q 7 3   ♡ K 9 6   ◇ K J 8 7   ♣ A 10

You have 17 HCP, so you bid the obvious 3NT without a care in the world. Where are your nine winners? Until dummy is tabled, no one could possibly know.

However, on hands which contain a long strong suit, you may be able to count your tricks during the auction. Playing tricks are defined as the number of tricks you expect to win on your own on offense.

If the losers in your long suit are easy to determine, **playing tricks = 13 minus the number of losers.**

You deal with both sides vulnerable. What's your call?

♠ Q J 10 9 8 7 6   ♡ 6   ◇ J 10 9 8   ♣ 5
With spades as trumps, you expect to lose 2 spades, 1 heart, 3 diamonds and 1 club trick. Because you have 7 losers, this hand has 6 playing tricks. That's all you need for a vulnerable 3♠ preempt. As for only 4 HCP — POINTS SCHMOINTS!

♠ A K Q J 8 5 4   ♡ 8 7   ◇ 9   ♣ A K 10
With spades as trumps, you are confident of winning 7 spades and 2 club tricks. You have as many quick tricks (4) as losers (4), and that's enough to open 2♣ despite having just 17 HCP.

Playing Tricks (continued)

West	North	East	South
—	—	—	1♢
Pass	1♡	Pass	???

♠ 5 4 3   ♡ 9   ♢ A K Q 9 7 5 4 3   ♣ A

Bid 3NT. With 9 playing tricks, any other action would be cowardly. If you're concerned about "what ifs" in spades or hearts, you are worrying too much. Your bid shows a good hand based on great diamonds.

West	North	East	South
—	—	Pass	1♡
Pass	1NT	Pass	???

♠ 9 5   ♡ A K J 10 8 6 5   ♢ —   ♣ K J 10 9

At most, you will lose 2 spade tricks, 1 heart and 2 clubs. With 8+ playing tricks and terrific intermediates, you must insist on game after partner's response. Bid 4♡.

West	North	East	South
—	—	—	1♠
Pass	2♠	3♣	???

♠ A K 10 8 6 5 4   ♡ 7 5 3   ♢ A   ♣ A 4

After partner's raise, you expect your spades to be solid. You therefore have 9 winners and 4 losers. If you bid the "obvious" 4♠, you need partner to cover one of your losers. But if you bid 3NT and partner passes (with a flat hand), you'll have no problem making your contract after the marked club lead. Sold!

100 Honors — Awesome

Any suit containing four honors can be bid as if it were one card longer than it really is.

West	North	East	South
—	—	1♣	???

♠ 8 ♡ A Q J 10 ◇ 6 4 3 2 ♣ A Q 9 7

Overcall 1♡. Any other action would make no sense. If partner raises you with three small hearts, nothing bad will happen.

West	North	East	South
—	—	—	1♡
Pass	1NT	Pass	???

♠ Q J 10 8 ♡ A K Q J 9 ◇ 8 5 4 ♣ 3

Rebid 2♡, whether or not you're playing 1NT Forcing. You should be delighted to bid this exquisite heart suit again. You'd need a much better hand for a 2♠ *reverse*.

West	North	East	South
—	—	1♠	Dbl
Pass	2♣	Pass	???

♠ 7 3 ♡ K Q J 10 ◇ A 9 8 4 ♣ A K J

Bid 2♡, promising at least 17 HCP and five hearts. Yes, you have only four hearts, but they are so lovely that you are treating hearts as a five-card suit.

Trump Suit Intermediates

With less than a 9-card fit in trumps, always take a close look at your trump intermediates.

Everyone is concerned about the quality of their trumps. After all, that is the one suit where it is impossible to throw away your losers.

In addition, players should also appreciate the number of trumps they hold. Each extra trump is one less for the opponents, and can make a big difference in the play.

However, appreciating your trump intermediates is much less obvious. For example:

Suppose you open 1♠, and partner raises you to 2♠. You're thinking about bidding on, but it's a close decision. You have a 5-card spade suit headed by the AQ. But what are your other three trumps? Here are some possibilities:

A Q 4 3 2   A Q 9 3 2   A Q 9 8 4

A Q 10 3 2   A Q 10 9 8

These holdings should not all be evaluated the same way. Facing a partner with three trumps, the difference between A Q 4 3 2 and A Q 10 9 8 is at least 1 point! For example, if partner has three small spades, you could easily lose an extra trick when you lack intermediates. And if the opponents' five trumps divide 4-1 (more than 30% of the time), you might even lose control of the hand.

Intermediates for Preempts and Overcalls

Your intermediates are also very important when considering whether to preempt or overcall.

You are dealer with neither side vulnerable.
Most players would be delighted to open 3♠ with:

♠ K J 10 9 8 7 6   ♡ 8   ◇ 6 5   ♣ 8 7 3

However, suppose you held:

♠ K J 6 5 4 3 2   ♡ 8   ◇ 6 5   ♣ 8 7 3

Would you still open 3♠? Many players would not.

If you do choose to preempt, as I would, you may very well buy the contract for 3♠. However, if partner tables a small singleton, the presence or absence of spade intermediates will make all the difference in the world.

With the first holding, you can't possibly lose more than two trump tricks, and on a good day, will only lose one.

With the second hand, you would not be surprised to lose three trump tricks, and if you get a 4-1 split, four losers are quite possible. In addition, when you get to dummy and lead a trump, you have an annoying blind guess. When your RHO follows with a small card, do you finesse the king or the jack? Yuck!

No wonder I love having intermediates in my long suits.

Preempts and Overcalls (continued)

Your RHO opens 1♡ with both sides vulnerable.
What's your call?

♠ K J 3 2   ♡ A Q 10 9   ◇ K 3   ♣ 8 5 4
Pass. You don't have any reason to bid.

♠ K J 10 9   ♡ A Q 3 2   ◇ K 2   ♣ 8 5 4
Overcall 1♠, happy to encourage partner to support spades
or lead that suit on defense.

♠ 7 4   ♡ A 5   ◇ K 7 6 4   ♣ A J 4 3 2
Pass. You have more to lose than to gain by overcalling
this moth-eaten suit.

♠ 7 4   ♡ A 5   ◇ K 7 6 4   ♣ A J 10 9 8
Overcall 2♣. Not a bad suit at all.

♠ Q J 6 5 4 3 2   ♡ 6 5   ◇ K 3 2   ♣ 6
Jump to 2♠. Since you have no intermediates, it's wise
to be cautious.

♠ Q J 10 9 8 7 6   ♡ 6 5   ◇ K 10 9   ♣ 6
Jump to 3♠. Vulnerable, schmulnerable.

♠ 9 5   ♡ 5   ◇ K J 4 3 2   ♣ K J 4 3 2
Pass. With these "empty" suits, you shouldn't jump to
2NT (Unusual Notrump) vulnerable.

♠ 9 5   ♡ 5   ◇ K J 10 9 8   ♣ K J 10 9 8
Bid 2NT. Two nice, chunky suits.

A Penny for My Thoughts

You are dealt: ♠ A K 9 8   ♡ Q 5 2   ♢ A J 10 8 3   ♣ 4

First impressions:
14 HCP   5-4-3-1 distribution   3 quick tricks

Location of Honors:
The ♠K should be upgraded because it is accompanied by the ♠A. This is reflected by counting an AK as the same two quick tricks as two aces.

With no other heart honors, the ♡Q must be downgraded. **Unaccompanied minor honors are questionable assets.** Of course, if partner bids hearts, it will be a lovely card.

Because the ♢J and ♢10 are accompanied by the ace in your 5-card diamond suit, they should be upgraded.

Distribution:
5-4-3-1 hands should always be well-regarded. Players who initially add for length will add a point for a five-card suit. Those who prefer to add for short suits, add two for the singleton. Whether you think this hand is worth 15 points or 16, it is definitely worth more than 14 points.

Suit Quality:
Because of the honors and length, your spade and diamond intermediates are well-placed. If partner has any honors in those suits, you have excellent chances to win extra tricks.

Summary: With many pluses and only 1 minus (♡Q), this hand is worth 1 or 2 points more than your initial count.

Pluses and Minuses

Here is a list of guidelines for determining whether your hand should be upgraded or downgraded. This does not mean that you need only memorize this page to become a better player; but keeping these points in mind will go a long way towards improving your hand evaluation.

Upgrades   Downgrades

Honor Cards

Upgrades	Downgrades
more than one ace	more than one queen more than one jack
honors in your long suit(s)	honors in short suit(s)
honors with other honors	isolated honors
honor(s) in partner's long suit	no help for partner's suit

Distribution

Upgrades	Downgrades
long suit	no 5+ card suit
second suit of 4+ cards	no second suit
short suits (suit contract)	flat hand (4–3–3–3 is worst)
finding a fit	misfit for partner's long suit
short in opponent's suit	length in opponent's suit

Suit Quality

Upgrades	Downgrades
3+ honors in longest suit	weak long suit(s)
intermediates in long suit(s)	no intermediates

Your Turn to Shine

For each set, rank the three hands: worst, middle, best. The answers for sets 2-4 can be found on the next page.

Set 1. Rank the hands. Also, would you open?

♠ Q J x x ♡ K J 10 ◇ x x x x x ♣ A   WORST
A terrible long suit and a not-so-hot singleton ace. Pass.

♠ A Q J x ♡ K 10 x ◇ J x x x x ♣ x   MIDDLE
You'd prefer that your longest suit be stronger.
I would open, but a pass would not be foolish.

♠ A J 10 x ♡ x x x ◇ K Q J x x ♣ x   BEST
All of your honors are in your two long suits. Open 1◇.

Set 2. Partner opens 1♡ and you raise to 2♡.
♠ Q x x x ♡ A x x ◇ Q x x x ♣ x x
♠ A x x x ♡ Q x x ◇ Q x x x ♣ x x
♠ A x x x ♡ x x x ◇ Q x x x ♣ Q x

Set 3. You are the dealer.
♠ K Q ♡ Q x x x ◇ K J x x ♣ K J x
♠ x x ♡ Q J x x ◇ A K J x ♣ A 10 x
♠ x x ♡ A K 10 x ◇ K J 10 x ♣ A x x

Set 4. Partner opens 1♡ and raises your 1♠ response to 2♠. Rank the hands. Also, what's your call?
♠ K Q J x ♡ x x ◇ 10 x x x ♣ A J x
♠ K x x x ♡ J ◇ K J x x ♣ Q J x x
♠ A Q J 10 ♡ A x ◇ x x x x ♣ x x x

Your Turn to Shine (Answers)

Set 2. Partner opens 1♡ and you raise to 2♡.

♠ Q x x x   ♡ A x x   ◇ Q x x x   ♣ x x   MIDDLE
Your two outside queens are unproven.

♠ A x x x   ♡ Q x x   ◇ Q x x x   ♣ x x   BEST
One of your queens (hearts) is now proven.

♠ A x x x   ♡ x x x   ◇ Q x x x   ♣ Q x   WORST
No trump honor and a dubious queen doubleton in clubs.

Set 3. You are the dealer.

♠ K Q   ♡ Q x x x   ◇ K J x x   ♣ K J x   WORST
In fact, this aceless, spotless mess is not strong enough to
open 1NT. I would open 1◇.

♠ x x   ♡ Q J x x   ◇ A K J x   ♣ A 10 x   MIDDLE

♠ x x   ♡ A K 10 x   ◇ K J 10 x   ♣ A x x   BEST
Two great red suits and 3 ½ quick tricks.

Set 4. Partner opens 1♡ and raises your 1♠ bid to 2♠.

♠ K Q J x   ♡ x x   ◇ 10 x x x   ♣ A J x   MIDDLE
Bid 3♠. You have enough to invite.

♠ K x x x   ♡ J   ◇ K J x x   ♣ Q J x x   WORST
I would pass. The only working honor is the ♠K.

♠ A Q J 10   ♡ A x   ◇ x x x x   ♣ x x x   BEST
Bid 4♠. All the right stuff.

The Rule of 20 — with Adjustments

When using the Rule of 20, always remember to evaluate and adjust.

In first or second seat, the Rule of 20 is a great way to determine whether or not to open borderline hands. Add the length of your two longest suits to your HCP. If the total is 20 or more, open one of a suit. With less than 20, either preempt (with a suitable hand), or pass. **However, your evaluation skills should come into play**

♠ 7 4   ♡ A Q 10 9 7   ◇ A 10 9 6   ♣ 8 6
5 hearts + 4 diamonds + 10 HCP = 19.
A total of 19 calls for a pass; but you should upgrade and open 1♡. Your high cards and intermediates are concentrated in your attractive long suits, you have 2½ quick tricks, and 2 aces + 2 tens are really worth 9½ HCP.

♠ K Q   ♡ J 6 5 4 2   ◇ Q J 6 2   ♣ Q J
5 hearts + 4 diamonds + 12 HCP = 21.
Pass. So many minuses. No aces, questionable holdings in spades and clubs, only 1 quick trick, and your longest suit is terrible. This hand is a pile of garbage.

♠ A Q 9 7 5 2   ♡ 7 4 2   ◇ —   ♣ K 10 9 7
6 spades + 4 clubs + 9 HCP = 19.
But open 1♠, not 2♠. The 4-card side suit often results in an extra trick, and you prefer 3-0 in the other suits to 2-1.

Keep in mind: The Rule of 20 does not reflect your third-longest suit. It's up to you to appreciate that 5-4-4-0 is better than 5-4-3-1, which is better than 5-4-2-2, etc.

Questions From The Readers

Dear Marty: I've read that you advocate opening 1NT with a 5-card major. Yesterday, at duplicate, I opened 1NT with:

♠ A 10 7   ♡ A 10 9 8 4   ◇ A 6 5   ♣ A 5

I'm sure you'll agree, but my partner needs to see it in black and white.   *Confident in Los Angeles*

Dear Overconfident: You are correct that I am happy to open 1NT with a 5-card major, but this hand is definitely too strong for 1NT. Let's see what The Computer Sez:

4 aces @ 4½ each = 18   2 tens @ 1/4 each = ½
Computer Total = 18½

And then there's the nice 5-card suit, which is clearly an asset. This hand is overqualified for 1NT — open 1♡.

Dear Marty: Please help us settle a bet. My husband loves your Rule of 20, and opened 1♣ in second seat with a lousy hand. I didn't agree. He held:

♠ J 7   ♡ Q J 6 5   ◇ K J   ♣ Q J 6 5 2

We've decided to let you resolve our bet. Who has to do the dishes next week?   *Joan in Reno*

Dear Joan: Enjoy your week off. He should have passed. With 5-4 in his long suits, he needed 11 HCP to hit 20. Four jacks should be downgraded to 3 HCP. Add 2 queens (3 HCP), and a king (3), and his true total was only 9 HCP. In addition, the ◇KJ and ♠Jx were not worth much.

What Should I Open?

With four diamonds and five clubs, some hands should open 1◇ or 1NT to avoid rebid problems.

1. With a strong hand, (17+ HCP or a gorgeous 16), there's no problem. Open the obvious 1♣, intending to reverse into diamonds.

   ♠ 7 ♡ A Q 9 ◇ K J 6 5 ♣ A K J 5 3
   ♠ A 9 5 ♡ 8 ◇ A K 8 6 ♣ A J 10 8 5

2. With 2-2 in the majors and 15-16 HCP, open 1NT despite the two doubletons.

   ♠ A J ♡ J 7 ◇ K Q 8 5 ♣ K Q 6 5 3
   ♠ K 4 ♡ K 4 ◇ A 10 8 5 ♣ A J 9 8 3

3. On all other hands with four diamonds and five clubs:
   if the diamonds are lovely, open 1◇;
   if the diamonds don't sparkle, open 1♣.

   Open 1◇ with:

   ♠ — ♡ K 9 8 5 ◇ A Q J 6 ♣ Q J 8 7 4
   ♠ Q 8 7 ♡ 6 ◇ A K 10 9 ♣ K 8 7 4 2

   Open 1♣ with:

   ♠ K ♡ K Q 7 ◇ Q 7 6 3 ♣ K J 9 7 4
   ♠ Q 7 ♡ A 9 ◇ J 7 6 5 ♣ A Q 7 5 3

Strong Enough to Open 2♣?

Opening 2♣ with a balanced hand is easy. Count your HCP, evaluate your hand, and if you're too strong to open 2NT, open 2♣.

Unbalanced hands are not so easy. How strong a hand do you need? Opinions vary. Here are mine:

- Open 2♣ with 9+ playing tricks and 4+ quick tricks.
- The number of HCP is not the key.
- When you have a second suit, avoid opening 2♣ with a long minor suit. After any response, opener must introduce his minor at the three level, which wastes bidding space, and often results in a messy auction.

♠ A K Q J 9 8 7 4   ♡ A   ◇ 8 ⁙   ♣ 7 5
Open 1♠. Nine playing tricks, but only three quick tricks.

♠ 8 7 3   ♡ A K Q J 6 2   ◇ A K Q   ♣ 3
Open 2♣. Nine playing tricks and four quick tricks.

♠ A K Q 6 3   ♡ A K Q J 2   ◇ 4 2   ♣ 7
Open 2♣. Four quick tricks, with lots of playing tricks in your two gorgeous major suits.

♠ A 6   ♡ A K 10 4   ◇ A K J 8 5 4   ♣ 5
Open 1◇. With a long *major* suit, you'd be happy to open 2♣. If you open 2♣ with this hand, your earliest chance to show your hearts would be at the four level.

♠ A 6   ♡ A 5   ◇ K 2   ♣ A K Q 7 6 5 3
Open 2♣. No second suit to worry about. You will show your clubs and then follow with 3NT.

Opener Raises Responder's Major

West	North	East	South
—	—	—	1♣
Pass	1♠	Pass	???

♠ A 10 6   ♡ 7 4   ◊ A 5 3   ♣ A 7 6 3 2

Bid 2♠, not 1NT. Hands with "aces and spaces" play much better in a suit than in notrump. Your holding in the unbid major also suggests avoiding notrump.

♠ A K 9 7   ♡ 4   ◊ 8 4 2   ♣ A Q 10 7 5

Bid 3♠, not 2♠. Once partner bids spades, this is NOT a minimum opening bid. 5-4-3-1 hands are wonderful, especially when your honors are in your long suits and partner has not bid your short suit.

♠ 7 5 4 2   ♡ Q 6   ◊ Q J   ♣ A K Q J 10

Bid 2♠, not 3♠. Other than your clubs, how ugly can you get? With only two prime cards, a single raise is enough.

♠ A J 10 5   ♡ 7 4   ◊ A 8   ♣ A K 9 8 6

Bid 4♠, not 3♠. Lovely trumps, a source of tricks (clubs), and three aces. No guarantees, but partner should have an excellent chance to make 4♠.

♠ J 6 5 4   ♡ A K 2   ◊ K J 3   ♣ K Q J

Bid 3♠, not 4♠. Weak trumps, 4-3-3-3, and only one ace, so take the low road. If responder declines your invitation, you'll have no regrets.

Fits and Misfits

Even with a strong hand, when you have a misfit, stop bidding ASAP. However, if the hand fits, bid 'em up.

West	North	East	South
—	—	—	1♡
Pass	1♠	Pass	2♣
Pass	2♠	Pass	???

♠ — ♡ A 9 7 5 3 ◇ K 8 6 4 ♣ A Q 10 3

Pass. This is obviously not the contract of your dreams, but don't make matters worse by bidding on.

♠ 3 ♡ K J 6 4 3 ◇ A K J ♣ K J 7 2

Pass. Despite your diamond strength and 16 HCP, don't bid 2NT — that invites 3NT. What suit will you develop in notrump? Having stoppers in all suits does not make a good notrump contract; you also need a source of tricks.

♠ A ♡ A 10 7 4 3 ◇ 8 6 2 ♣ A K J 9

Bid 3♠. Your singleton ace is adequate support for partner's 6-card suit, and your four quick tricks represent four winners.

♠ J 10 8 ♡ A 9 8 6 4 ◇ 4 ♣ A K 5 2

Bid 4♠. Only 12 HCP, but now you're talking. You have a superb fit for spades, and partner should be able to ruff a diamond or two. All of your honors are working overtime.

Open 1NT?

Not all balanced hands with 15-17 HCP have the right strength to open 1NT.

Have I lost my mind? You be the judge. You hold:

♠ Q 6 4 2 ♡ K Q J ◇ Q J 5 2 ♣ K J

I am aware that many players would open 1NT. However, it would not occur to me. An average 1NT opening has 3 to 3½ quick tricks. This abomination has a mere 1½. I am also not impressed by the lack of aces or spot cards. I would open 1◇, and treat the hand as the equivalent of 13 HCP. By the way, using our computer-aided revised point-count, (A = 4½, K = 3, Q = 1½, J = ¾, 10 = ¼), the total for this mess is 12 ¾.

On the other hand, take a look at:

♠ K 10 5 ♡ A 6 ◇ A Q 10 9 7 ♣ A 6 2

Vive la différence. 4 quick tricks, not to mention 3 aces, 2 tens, and a lovely 5-card suit. Please don't tell me that you would open 1NT. With all of these pluses, you should open 1◇ and jump to 2NT after a major suit response. What does the computer say this time? A hefty 18 ¾ (which doesn't even reflect the 5-card suit).

After 1NT - 2NT

When you open 1NT and partner invites game by raising, the final decision is yours. With 15 or 17 HCP, the answer is easy; but with 16, you're in the middle. To bid or not to bid? As always, the key to making informed decisions is to practice good hand evaluation.

West	North	East	South
—	—	—	1NT
Pass	2NT	Pass	???

♠ K 3   ♡ A K 10 9   ◇ K Q J 3   ♣ 6 4 3
Bid 3NT. This is clear-cut. You love your heart intermediates, and the ◇3 increases your trick-taking potential in that suit.

♠ K Q J   ♡ J 7 5 3   ◇ A Q   ♣ K 7 5 3
Pass. Easy as pie. You have no spot cards, and more strength in your short suits than in your longer ones.

♠ K Q 4   ♡ A 7 5   ◇ K 3   ♣ A 10 8 4 2
Bid 3NT. The 5-card suit makes all the difference.

♠ Q J 10   ♡ K Q 3   ◇ A J 8 4   ♣ K 9 3
Pass. I have seen worse 16-counts. You do have an ace and a few intermediates. However, you are 4-3-3-3.
Most hands with 4-3-3-3 should decline invitations.

♠ A 7 6   ♡ A J 7 3   ◇ A K 10 4   ♣ 5 3
Bid 3NT. The Computer Sez: this hand is worth 17½ HCP. I'm also impressed with the four quick tricks.
Most hands with three aces should accept invitations.

Support with Support

When you open 1NT and partner transfers, you should usually jump with four trumps.

When you accept the transfer, you are not showing support. You are just following orders, and may have a doubleton in responder's suit. When opener does have four-card support, he should do something dramatic, and jumping opposite partner's possible Yarborough certainly qualifies. You don't need 17 HCP for this jump; just a hand that "looks good" for playing in responder's suit.

West	West	East	East
♠ A Q 10 6	1NT	2♡	♠ J 8 7 4 3
♡ A 8 6	3♠	4♠	♡ 7 3
◇ 6 2	Pass		◇ A 8 7 5 3
♣ A J 9 2			♣ 5

West may have only 15 HCP, but has a terrific hand in support of spades. East had not considered game, but once opener showed great support, he correctly reevaluated his 5-5 distribution and ◇ A.

The reward for a well-bid hand was a nice game bonus when West played carefully. Once he realized there was no reason to draw trumps, making 4♠ was a walk in the park.

By the way: If opener has 3-card support, he should avoid jumping, even with a maximum hand. Unless your side has a lot of strength, The LAW of Total Tricks suggests that rushing to the three level with only eight trumps is a losing proposition.

After Partner Opens 1NT

West	North	East	South
Pass	1NT	Pass	???

♠ Q 7 5   ♡ K J 4   ◇ Q 8 3   ♣ 7 6 4 2

Pass. No aces and no intermediates. Not only are you 4-3-3-3, but your 4-card suit is awful. Forget about 3NT. **When partner opens 1NT, don't always bid with 8 HCP.**

♠ 6 4   ♡ 7 5 4   ◇ K J 9 6   ♣ A 10 6 4

Bid 2NT. This hand is much better than the one above. Both of your 4-card suits are promising.

♠ 5 4   ♡ 10 9 7   ◇ K J 10 9   ♣ A 10 9 8

Bid 3NT. Three tens and three nines — now you're cooking. Appreciate all of these intermediates; you won't get them very often.

♠ A J 5   ♡ K J 2   ◇ Q 6 4 3   ♣ A 7 2

Bid 3NT. 15 HCP with 4-3-3-3 distribution is not enough for slam opposite a 15-17 1NT.

♠ Q 7 6 3   ♡ J 6   ◇ Q J 7   ♣ Q 5 4 2

Pass. What a mess! Don't bid Stayman, don't bid 2NT, don't bid anything at all. Even if you have a 4-4 spade fit, you are missing too many aces and kings to make a game.

♠ A 7 6 3   ♡ 6 5   ◇ 7 4 2   ♣ A 5 4 2

Bid 2♣. This hand is a lot better than the previous one.

♠ 10 8 5 3   ♡ 8 5 3   ◇ A K 10 8 4   ♣ 5

Bid 2♣. This hand is definitely worth more than 7 HCP. If partner bids 2◇ or 2♡, rebid 2NT. If he bids 2♠, jump to 4♠.

After Opener Rebids His Suit

When partner shows a 6-card suit, your holding in his suit becomes critical.

West	North	East	South
Pass	1♣	Pass	1♡
Pass	2♣	Pass	???

♠ A 8   ♡ 10 7 5 3   ◊ 8 5 4 2   ♣ A 9 2

Bid 3♣. Your two aces and club fit offer definite prospects for 3NT.

♠ K J 4 2   ♡ Q 7 6 4 2   ◊ K Q 5   ♣ 3

Pass. A (small) singleton in partner's 6-card suit should cause you to seriously downgrade your hand. Being aceless doesn't help either. Regardless of what partner has, any game is very unlikely.

♠ K 7 4 2   ♡ J 6 4 2   ◊ A Q 5   ♣ J 3

Bid 2NT. After partner rebids clubs, this is a much better hand than the previous example, even though both have 11 HCP. The club fit makes all the difference.

♠ K 7 4   ♡ A 6 4 2   ◊ A 5   ♣ 9 7 6 3

Bid 3NT. Your 4-card fit for partner's 6-card suit and three prime cards make this bid a standout.

♠ 8 3   ♡ A 7 6 5 3   ◊ A 8 5   ♣ K 9 2

Bid 2◊. You can't bid notrump without a spade stopper, but with three prime cards, you are too strong to bid an invitational 3♣. If opener reveals a stopper in the unbid spade suit by bidding 2NT, you will raise to 3NT.

I Changed My Mind

Unexpected developments during the auction may cause you to drastically alter your evaluation of a hand.

It was late in a close match of the semi-finals of the 1982 Vanderbilt. With both sides vulnerable, I sat South and picked up:

♠ 8 5 3   ♡ K J 6 4   ◇ J 2   ♣ A Q 7 6

My partner opened 1♠ and I responded 1NT (Forcing), treating my hand as a 3-card limit raise. If opener rebid two of a minor, I intended to jump to 3♠ to show my invitational raise. The auction continued:

West	North	East	South
Pass	1♠	Pass	1NT
Dbl	Pass	2◇	???

Because he passed originally, West's vulnerable takeout double had to be based on spade shortness. Therefore, East had at least four spades, and given my weak spades, he was probably sitting behind my partner with spade strength as well.

Accordingly, I changed my mind and bid 2♠, bidding as if I had a very weak hand. Everyone passed, and my partner limped home with eight tricks. At the other table, N-S went down two in 4♠ doubled. Partner held:

♠ A K 7 4 2   ♡ Q 7 2   ◇ A 5   ♣ J 5 3

Raising Opener's Major

West	North	East	South
—	1♠	Pass	???

For each hand, evaluate whether your hand is worth a single raise or a limit raise. It doesn't matter whether you play Standard, Bergen Raises, 1NT Forcing, etc.

♠ 5 4 2   ♡ Q J   ◊ Q J 5 3   ♣ K J 6 2
Single raise. You have six honor cards, but their quality leaves much to be desired. This hand is totally soft.

♠ A 8 6 4   ♡ 7 3   ◊ A 9 7 5 4   ♣ 8 5
Limit raise. That's more like it. The value of these honors is not in doubt.

♠ J 7 5 3   ♡ K 3   ◊ Q J 3   ♣ Q 7 6 3
Single raise. Despite the four trumps, a lot of your points are really "schmoints." Only the ♠J is proven.

♠ A 9 7   ♡ Q 7 5 4   ◊ K 6 5 3   ♣ 8 6
Single raise. Your red-suit honors are unproven.

♠ Q 9 7   ♡ A K 8 4   ◊ 7 6 5 3   ♣ 8 6
Limit raise. All three honors are working.

♠ Q J 10 4   ♡ —   ◊ K 7 6 5 3 2   ♣ 9 7 2
Bid 4♠. You have too much offense for either a single raise or a limit raise. In addition, you have virtually no defense against a heart contract. If your LHO wants to bid hearts, let him do so at the five level.

After Opener Raises Your Major

West	North	East	South
Pass	1◇	Pass	1♠
Pass	2♠	Pass	???

North's raise shows a minimum opening bid with a spade fit. He may have only 3-card support with a ruffing value.

♠ J 5 4 2 ♡ K Q J ◇ Q ♣ Q 6 5 3 2
Pass. Not a bad hand, but all the signs are wrong. You have terrible trumps, a misfit for opener's suit, a weak long suit, and "too much" strength in your 3-card heart suit.

♠ K J 10 7 5 ♡ J 6 3 ◇ K 6 4 ♣ K 8
Bid 3♠. A straightforward invitation to game.

♠ Q 9 5 4 ♡ A J 6 ◇ Q 8 3 ♣ A 7 6
Bid 3NT. Opener will pass with 3-card support, and bid 4♠ if he has four spades.

♠ Q J 9 5 ♡ 8 5 ◇ A 8 4 ♣ A Q 5 3
Bid 3♣, exploring for the best contract. This bid is forcing for one round.

♠ K 10 8 6 5 2 ♡ 5 ◇ 8 4 ♣ A 9 5 3
Bid 4♠. Once opener raises spades, you are looking good.

♠ K 8 6 5 4 3 ♡ 8 6 ◇ A Q ♣ A 10 6
Bid 3♣. Don't make the lazy bid of 4♠. Slam is quite possible. After all, you belong in 7NT if partner holds:

♠ A 9 7 2 ♡ A 9 ◇ K J 10 4 3 ♣ 5 3

She Who Knows, Goes

If all you need from partner to make a game is a minimum hand with the right card(s) — bid 'em up.

The easiest time to apply this principle is when partner has preempted. She has limited her HCP and given you a good picture of her hand — you need little else.

West	North	East	South
—	3♢	Pass	???

♠ 10 7 5 4 2　♡ A 4 3　♢ K 7 2　♣ A 3

Bid 3NT. As long as partner has seven diamonds headed by the ace, you're looking good.

West	North	East	South
Pass	2♡	Pass	???

♠ A 5 2　♡ K 7 6　♢ A K 10 8 7　♣ 9 6

Bid 4♡. All partner needs is a good heart suit and three clubs (so you can get a ruff). If not, your tenth trick may come from diamonds. A more delicate approach (2NT) is a waste of time.

By the way: Some players make the mistake of hoping that partner has perfect cards **and a maximum hand.** That is not good bridge; it is greed.

Responding to Partner's Double

West	North	East	South
1◇	Dbl	Pass	???

♠ A Q 10 8 5   ♡ 4   ◇ 8 6 5   ♣ 9 7 5 3
Bid 2♠, showing 9-11 points with spades as trumps.

♠ A J 10 9   ♡ 7 4   ◇ 8 6 5   ♣ K J 5 3
Bid 2♠. You don't need a 5-card suit to jump.
Your spades are chunky, and once partner promised clubs
(by doubling 1◇), your club honors are working.

♠ A J 10 9   ♡ 7 4   ◇ K J 6 5   ♣ 6 5 3
Bid 1♠. Your diamond honors are not worth much
because the opening bidder's diamonds are behind you,
and partner said he was short in that suit.

♠ A K 9 7 6 4   ♡ 9   ◇ 5 4 2   ♣ A J 3
Cue-bid 2◇, and then jump in spades. If partner has 0-1
diamond with good values, a spade slam is quite possible.

♠ K 9 7 6 5 3   ♡ 7 4   ◇ 7 3   ♣ 6 5 3
Bid 3♠. This double jump shows a weak hand with a
6-card suit. Once partner promised at least three spades by
doubling, you're delighted to follow The LAW (of Total
Tricks) and bid to the three level with nine trumps.

♠ J 10 9 4 3   ♡ K 9 8 7 2   ◇ 7   ♣ A 6
Bid 4◇. This seat-of-the-pants jump cue-bid asks partner
to bid game in the major of his choice.

♠ K 9 8 6 4 3   ♡ A 10 9 2   ◇ 7   ♣ 8 6
Bid 4♠. 6-4, bid more, especially with your known fit.

Bigger May Not be Better

Marty Sez: "Most players fall in love with big hands, but have no use for hands that are weak." Keep in mind that appearances can be deceiving. You must always listen carefully to the auction. Sometimes, a terrific hand can turn into a mirage.

West	North	East	South
—	—	—	2♣
Pass	2♦	Pass	2♠
Pass	3♣*	Pass	3♦
Pass	3♠	Pass	???

*3♣ = second negative

♠ K J 6 4 3   ♡ A K Q   ♢ A K J 3   ♣ K

You have 24 HCP, a bit more than your usual allotment. Your first three bids are automatic. Partner shows a very bad hand (0-3 HCP) with his 3♣ bid. Once you bid 3♦, he is forced to bid again. His 3♠ bid is merely a preference, and doesn't even say that he likes spades. If he really liked spades, he could have jumped to four.

Knowing that partner doesn't have points, and that he might have been forced to bid 3♠ with a worthless doubleton, you should pass.

For those who like to know, partner held:

♠ 9 2   ♡ 8 7 6 4   ♢ 8 5 4   ♣ J 9 6 2

Smaller May be Better

Sometimes, a weak hand can turn into solid gold.

Here's your chance to demonstrate that you can get the most out of a lousy hand. Both sides are vulnerable.

West	North	East	South
—	1♡	Pass	Pass
2♠	3♣	Pass	???

♠ 6 4 3 2 ♡ K 10 9 ◇ 7 5 4 3 ♣ 6 4

How many hearts do you bid with your modest 3 HCP?
You should jump to four! Partner is willing to contract for nine tricks after hearing that you have nothing. Your hand includes no less than four positive features: two heart honors, the third heart and the doubleton club.

Partner's hand: ♠ J ♡ A Q J 8 6 ◇ 9 6 ♣ A K 10 8 3

West	North	East	South
—	1◇	Pass	1♠
Pass	2♣	Pass	2♠
Pass	3♣	Pass	???

♠ J 10 9 8 7 5 ♡ 4 ◇ A 9 ♣ Q 10 9 3

Partner has 5-5 (at least) in the minors. He is probably void in spades, since he is unwilling to play in your major.
When you bid 2♠, you rated to have strength in spades and nothing else. Instead, you have 4-card club support with two honors, an ace in his first suit and a singleton.
Therefore, you should jump all the way to 5♣.

Partner's hand: ♠ — ♡ J 8 5 ◇ K Q 7 5 2 ♣ A K J 7 4

A Special Offer on a Special Bridge Cruise

Even if a bridge cruise does not appeal to you, here is an unprecedented offer. Mention this cruise to your friends and fellow bridge players. **For _each_ person you refer who takes the cruise, I will pay YOU $25 _even if you don't go along_. There is no limit, and you can count yourself if you do decide to join us.**
For details, call Marty toll-free at 1-800-386-7432.

Take a Caribbean Cruise with Marty Bergen

November 2 - 9, 2003

Your special vacation awaits! Each morning, Marty presents a 2½ hour lecture. He will also be available for questions and private lessons. As much duplicate bridge as you care to play, plus all the activities, entertainment and ambiance that you would expect to find on a cruise ship.

Ship sails from Ft. Lauderdale, Florida on Sunday, November 2. Travel aboard Holland America's 5-star ship _Maasdam_ to St. Thomas, Nassau, Puerto Rico, U.S. Virgin Islands, and the Bahamas, among other exotic ports. Ship returns to Ft. Lauderdale on Sunday, November 9.

Early booking bonus:
Book passage by Jan. 31, 2003 and receive $50 off.

**If you would like to receive flyers
or if you have any questions about the cruise,
call Bruce Travel (800-367-9980).**

In order to participate in bridge activities,
you must book the cruise through Bruce Travel.

Hardcover Books by Marty Bergen

MARTY SEZ	$17.95
MARTY SEZ – VOLUME 2	$17.95
POINTS SCHMOINTS!	$19.95
More POINTS SCHMOINTS!	$19.95
Schlemiel...Schlimazel? Mensch (non-bridge)	$14.95

Softcover Books by Marty Bergen

Understanding 1NT Forcing		$5.95
Hand Evaluation: Points, Schmoints!		$7.95
Introduction to Negative Doubles		$6.95
Negative Doubles		$9.95
Better Bidding With Bergen 1 – Non-Competitive		$11.95
Better Bidding With Bergen 2 – Competitive		$11.95
Marty's Reference book on Conventions	~~$9.95~~	$7.00

CDs by Marty Bergen

POINTS SCHMOINTS!	~~$29.95~~	$25

New interactive version of the award-winning book.

Marty Sez...	~~$24.95~~	$20

114 of Bergen's best bridge secrets.

Software By Fred Gitelman

Bridge Master 2000	~~$59.95~~	$48

"Best software ever created for improving your declarer play."

• • UNPRECEDENTED OFFER • •

If your purchase of Marty's hardcover books exceeds $25, mention this book and receive a 50% discount!

Personalized autographs available upon request.

Software by Mike Lawrence

Counting at Bridge $34.95 $30
Shows you ways to gather and use information.

Private Bridge Lessons: Vol. 1, Vol. 2 $34.95 $30 each
Declarer techniques that everyone needs to know.

Defense $34.95 $30
Avoid errors and take as many tricks as possible.

Two Over One $34.95 $30
Many hands to maximize your game and slam bidding.

Conventions $60.00 $48
A must for every partnership.

CDs By Larry Cohen

Play Bridge With Larry Cohen
"One of the best products to come along in years. Easy-to-use."

Days 1, 2, and 3 $29.95 $26 each

• • **FREE SHIPPING ON ALL SOFTWARE** • •
(in the U.S.)

ORDERING   INFORMATION

To place an order, call Marty toll-free at
1-800-386-7432
checks and credit cards are welcome

9 River Chase Terrace, Palm Beach Gardens, FL 33418

S&H is $3 per order. FREE shipping (US) with any hardcover book.